TABLE OF CONT[ENTS]

MW01102451

Encouraging Interest

Help students to develop an understanding and appreciation for character education themes through reading stories and chapter books that demonstrate positive character traits. The teacher may also wish to keep an ongoing bulletin board display that focuses on a specific character trait where students can display school work, projects, magazines, articles, etc.

Black Line Masters and Graphic Organizers

Encourage students to use the black line masters and graphic organizers to present information, reinforce important concepts and to extend opportunities for learning. The graphic organizers will help students focus on important ideas, or make direct comparisons.

Role-Playing

Role-playing offers an excellent opportunity for students to become sensitive to how others feel in different situations and to develop empathy. Be sure to introduce role-playing only after class members become familiar and comfortable with each other. In addition, set rules for role-playing to prevent inappropriate behaviour. In order for students to get the most out of role-playing, include:

- an enactment of the scenario presented
- a discussion and analysis of the scenario presented
- further role-playing of alternatives
- drawing conclusions regarding the scenario presented

Chalkboard Publishing © 2008

SELF-ESTEEM/PRIDE

Self-Esteem: to demonstrate a positive opinion of yourself
Pride: delight or satisfaction in your accomplishments, achievements and status

Strengths and Weaknesses

Have students complete a web graphic organizer to show their strengths, and another web to show their weaknesses they think they need to improve on. Reinforce the ideas that everyone has strengths and weaknesses.

Discussion Starters

- How do you feel when you do something well?
- Do you think it is o.k. to have things to improve on?
- Pick one thing you would like to improve. What are the steps in order to improve?

Student of the Week

Promote self- esteem and instill pride in students by selecting a "Student of the Week". This will also encourage students to learn more about their classmates and to create a community. Dedicate a bulletin board display with the student's information, pictures and schoolwork. The teacher may also wish to include written notes from the other students that compliment or recognize the student chosen for "Student of the Week".

Celebrating Students

Acknowledge and celebrate children's accomplishments and positive qualities on an ongoing basis using the various certificates provided in this teacher resource. Keep track of which certificates have been handed to whom in order to watch out for certain behaviors or accomplishments for certain students. Certificates can be given out in the moment, or the teacher may wish to hold a regular class meeting to recognize students.

Dealing with Peer Pressure

As a whole group, discuss peer pressure – pressure from people your own age to do things you normally wouldn't do on your own. Peer pressure can be positive or negative. Create a class T- Chart and list examples of positive and negative peer pressure.

Discussion Starters

- Why do you think people like to belong to a group?
- What does it take to stand up against negative peer pressure?
- Have you ever experienced negative peer pressure where you almost or did do something you did not want to do? If so, what happened and how did it make you feel?
- Have you ever experienced positive peer pressure where you tried something new? If so, what happened and how did make you feel?

Dealing with Stress

Students have to deal with stress just like adults. Many children not only have the responsibility of schoolwork, but also extra curricular activities, and family chores or responsibilities. With so many activities on the go, children might not have time to relax and take time for themselves. As a result, students may be tired, overwhelmed and worry if they don't complete everything they need to do. Use a web graphic organizer brainstorm ideas for dealing with stress and worries. For example, listening to music, exercise, making a schedule with a list they can check off as they complete things or getting enough sleep,

Discussion Starters

- What does the term "stressed" mean?
- How does it feel to be stressed?
- Do you ever worry about things? If so, what are some examples?
- Who can you talk with if you are worried about something?

SELF-ESTEEM DISCUSSION STARTERS

SELF-ESTEEM DISCUSSION STARTER

What is self- esteem?

Explain your thinking.

SELF-ESTEEM DISCUSSION STARTER

If someone brags or shows off what do you think that means about their self-esteem?

Explain your thinking.

SELF-ESTEEM DISCUSSION STARTER

When was the last time you thought something positive about yourself?

Explain your thinking.

SELF-ESTEEM DISCUSSION STARTER

How can trying something new help you feel good about yourself?

Explain your thinking.

SELF-ESTEEM DISCUSSION STARTER

Are there people who influence your opinion of yourself?

If yes, who and why?

SELF-ESTEEM DISCUSSION STARTER

What activities do you participate in that help you feel good about yourself?

Explain your thinking.

SELF-ESTEEM DISCUSSION STARTERS

SELF-ESTEEM DISCUSSION STARTER

Do you think it is a good idea to compare yourself to other people?

Explain your thinking.

SELF-ESTEEM DISCUSSION STARTER

Name something you like about yourself.

Explain your thinking.

SELF-ESTEEM DISCUSSION STARTER

How do you feel when you are given a compliment?

Explain your thinking.

SELF-ESTEEM DISCUSSION STARTER

Think about a time when you were feeling bad about yourself and then felt better.

What changed your feelings?

SELF-ESTEEM DISCUSSION STARTER

What can you do to help someone you know who's feeling bad about himself or herself?

Explain your thinking.

SELF-ESTEEM DISCUSSION STARTER

Whose opinion should matter the most to you?

Explain your thinking.

SHARING OUR PRIDE

Write a paragraph inside the balloon to share something that you are proud of.

ANALYZING ADVERTISEMENTS

Cut out and paste in the space below an advertisement that promotes good self-esteem.

Why did you choose this advertisement. Explain your thinking.

_____

_____

_____

_____

_____

PERSEVERANCE/DILIGENCE

Perseverance: determined to work hard at something, without giving up despite difficulties or setbacks

Diligence: persistent effort

Perseverance/Diligence

As a class, discuss with students what they think perseverance and diligence means. Also discuss how an athlete might show perseverance and diligence in order to acquire the skills necessary to become a champion. List the ways on a graphic web organizer. Next, have students complete a graphic web organizer to show how one the following requires perseverance:

- learning to play an instrument
- learning a new language
- learning to dance
- learning to sing
- a personal experience of their choosing

Setting Personal Goals

Have students set personal goals. Encourage students to persevere and to achieve their goals:

- Affirm to students your confidence that they can achieve their goals
- Give students honest feedback on what students are doing well and what they need to work on
- If a task seems overwhelming to a student, break it down into smaller more manageable parts
- Let students know that it is "ok" if something is not easy, and they can work through obstacles
- Stress the importance of "finishing what you have started"
- Talk about your own experiences
- Celebrate accomplishments and have students express how they feel when achieving their goal

Developing Good Work Habits

Help students take responsibility for their learning. Encourage students to self–assess their daily work habits using kid friendly and easy to understand criteria. The "How Am I Doing?" rubric provided in this teacher resource will clarify what makes a good piece of work exemplary and the qualities of an excellent student.

People Who Have Shown By Example

Provide for students a list of historical figures and other people who have set a good example of perseverance/diligence to accomplish a goal, such as one of Canada's explorers, or Terry Fox. Then have students complete a research poster, biography report or brochure, on that person.

* If possible, the teacher may also wish to invite a person from the community who has accomplished something in spite of a disability or other obstacles through perseverance.

PERSEVERANCE DISCUSSION STARTER

What does perseverance mean?
What does diligence mean?

Give examples.

PERSEVERANCE DISCUSSION STARTER

Why do you think some people
give up and stop trying to
accomplish their goal(s)?

Explain your thinking.

PERSEVERANCE DISCUSSION STARTER

Do you think attitude has anything
to do with success?

Explain your thinking.

PERSEVERANCE DISCUSSION STARTER

How do you think your
self-esteem affects your ability to
accomplish a goal?

Explain your thinking.

PERSEVERANCE DISCUSSION STARTER

Would you rather set low goals
that are easy to accomplish
for yourself or high goals that
are more challenging?

Explain your thinking.

PERSEVERANCE DISCUSSION STARTER

Is there an area in your life
you need to show
more perseverance?

Explain your thinking.

PROMOTE PERSEVERANCE

Create a slogan for a t-shirt to promote perseverance.

PERSEVERANCE SURVEY

People succeed when they persevere with their goals. Here are some ways you can show perseverance. Take this survey and think about how you persevere to accomplish your goals.

	Always	Sometimes	Never
I strive to do my best.			
I set a goal and stay focused on it.			
I don't give up if something becomes difficult.			
I don't postpone doing things.			
I am self- disciplined.			
I learn from mistakes, and failures.			

Do you think you demonstrate perseverance? Explain your thinking.

_____

_____

_____

_____

WORK HABITS SURVEY

Good work habits help people get their work done. Here are some examples of good work habits. Take this survey and think about your work habits.

	Always	Sometimes	Never
I complete my work on time and with care.			
I have good time management skills.			
I follow directions.			
I keep my materials organized.			
I take responsibility for my learning.			

Do you think you have good work habits? Explain your thinking.

_____

_____

_____

_____

GOAL SETTING

My goal _____

Why did you choose this goal? _____

List the steps to achieve this goal:

_____

_____

_____

_____

_____

_____

_____

The date you want to achieve your goal by: _____

How will you know if you achieved your goal?

_____

RESPONSIBILITY/TRUSTWORTHINESS

Responsibility: to carry out a duty or task carefully and thoroughly; be able to count on, depend, or trust
Trustworthiness: having the confidence of others

Responsibilities At Home

Encourage students to think about their own role in their family. What responsibilities do they have? Some responsibilities may be chores like cleaning up the dishes or vacuuming. Other responsibilities include following the rules set by their parents or caregivers. Next, ask students to think about special contributions each family member makes to their family. Record the student responses on a chart. Put checkmarks or tally marks to show repeat answers. What are the special responsibilities of owning a pet?

Responsibilities At School

As a whole group, brainstorm and list the responsibilities of a student. Ideas may include getting to class on time, keeping materials organized, having homework complete and contributing to class discussions. Ask students if they think they have a responsibility to act as good role models for younger students.

Time Management

As a class make a list of obligations that students have at home, at school and outside of school. Obligations may include chores, lessons, extra-curricular activities and homework. Ask students what they think "time management" means. Do they think it is important to include time in their schedule to relax? Who is responsible for managing their time? Do they think they can manage their time well without help? Have students complete the "Managing My Time" worksheet. Once finished, discuss how many obligations students had for the week. In addition, discuss if students managed to include activities of their choice.

Making Responsible Decisions

Encourage students to think about whether something is right or wrong before making a choice of how they will proceed in different situations. Role-play different scenarios. Compare and discuss what happens in each scenario with students who choose to do the "right thing" and with students who choose to do the "wrong thing". How would students feel after each decision? What are the consequences?

Brain Stretch For Students:

1. What can you think about before deciding if doing something is right or wrong?
2. What do you think would happen if nobody cared about doing the "right thing"?
3. Do you agree with "finder's keepers, loser's weepers"? Explain your thinking.

Trustworthiness

Discuss with students how they can show trustworthiness through their actions in their everyday life. Encourage students to think about how people rely on trust in order to make things work or get done at home, at school and in the community. What would happen if we lived in a world where people couldn't trust each other? How do you know that someone is trustworthy?

Chalkboard Publishing © 2008

RESPONSIBILITY DISCUSSION STARTERS

RESPONSIBILITY DISCUSSION STARTER

What are the characteristics of a responsible person?

Explain your thinking.

RESPONSIBILITY DISCUSSION STARTER

In what ways do you show you're responsible at home?

Explain your thinking.

RESPONSIBILITY DISCUSSION STARTER

In what ways do you show you're responsible at school?

Explain your thinking.

RESPONSIBILITY DISCUSSION STARTER

In what ways do you show you're responsible when you're out in the community?

Explain your thinking.

RESPONSIBILITY DISCUSSION STARTER

What does responsibility have to do with growing up?

Explain your thinking.

RESPONSIBILITY DISCUSSION STARTER

Is being responsible always easy?

Why or why not?

RESPONSIBILITY DISCUSSION STARTERS

RESPONSIBILITY DISCUSSION STARTER

Do you consider yourself to be a responsible person?

Explain your thinking.

RESPONSIBILITY DISCUSSION STARTER

Do you think people should take responsibility for their actions?

Why or why not?

RESPONSIBILITY DISCUSSION STARTER

Do you think being considered a responsible or an irresponsible person can affect a person's self-esteem?

Explain your thinking.

RESPONSIBILITY DISCUSSION STARTER

What are some of the responsibilities children your age have?

Explain your thinking.

RESPONSIBILITY DISCUSSION STARTER

What are some of the responsibilities adults have?

Explain your thinking.

RESPONSIBILITY DISCUSSION STARTER

What are the benefits from being a responsible person?

Explain your thinking.

RESPONSIBILITY SURVEY

Responsibility shows that you are dependable. Here are some ways you can show responsibility. Take this survey and think about how responsible you are.

	Always	Sometimes	Never
I take responsibility for my actions.			
I take responsibility to complete my schoolwork on time and with care.			
I am reliable and dependable.			
I do what needs to be done without someone reminding me.			
I make responsible decisions.			
I don't make excuses or blame others.			
I follow through on my commitments?			

Do you think you are a responsible person? Explain your thinking.

_____

_____

_____

_____

MANAGING YOUR TIME WISELY

A part of being responsible is being able to manage your time wisely. List the activities, chores, lessons, homework or other plans you are committed to doing outside of school and on weekends. At the end of each day, underline all the responsibilities you have completed.

Sunday	
Monday	
Tuesday	
Wednesday	
Thursday	
Friday	
Saturday	

TRUSTWORTHINESS SURVEY

People get along better when they are trustworthy. Here are some ways you can show trustworthiness. Take this survey and think about if you are trustworthy.

	Always	Sometimes	Never
I follow through on my commitments.			
I keep my promises.			
I don't cheat.			
I tell the truth.			
I obey the law.			
I can keep a secret.			

Do you think you are a trustworthy person? Explain your thinking.

_____

_____

_____

_____

FAMILIES WORK TOGETHER

Think about your role in your family. What are your responsibilities? How do you help? Complete the chart to show how family members have different responsibilities.

FAMILY MEMBER	RESPONSIBILITIES

RESPONSIBILITY AND YOU

What responsibilities do you feel you personally have for:

1. YOURSELF

2. YOUR FAMILY

3. YOUR COMMUNITY

4. THE WORLD

BE AN ADVICE COLUMNIST

Pretend you are the advice columnist for a kids' magazine. Read the following letters and write a letter of advice for each.

Dear Advisor,

My friends have told me that I have to steal something in order to be in their special group. If I don't do it, they say they won't be my friend. I want them to still be my friends, but I don't want to steal!

What should I do?

Dear Advisor,

My friend Dave wants to me to try out for the school soccer team with him. I really like to play soccer, but I don't want to embarrass myself.

What should I do?

Dear Advisor,

All my friends have already kissed somebody. I feel like I am the only one left. I don't feel like I belong around my friends. All they do is talk about kissing. Should I just kiss someone to get it over with?

What should I do?

Dear Advisor,

I really want to be in the school choir. My friends say I have a great voice and should try out. My friends said they would come with me and try out too. I still feel nervous.

What should I do?

Dear Advisor,

I am really good at math and we have a test soon. My friend wants to cheat off me. He says that if I am his real friend I will let him. I don't think that is right.

What should I do?

Dear Advisor,

I am in a new class this year. My new friends in my class don't like my best friend. They said I have to choose between my best friend and them.

What should I do?

TRUSTWORTHINESS DISCUSSION STARTERS

TRUSTWORTHINESS DISCUSSION STARTER

What does it mean to be trustworthy?

Give examples.

TRUSTWORTHINESS DISCUSSION STARTER

Do you think trust plays an important part in a friendship?

Explain your thinking.

TRUSTWORTHINESS DISCUSSION STARTER

A friend trusts you with a secret and tells you not to tell someone. What might happen if you go ahead and tell someone anyway?

Explain your thinking.

TRUSTWORTHINESS DISCUSSION STARTER

You have just trusted a friend with a secret, but then they told someone else. How would you feel? What would you do?

Explain your thinking.

TRUSTWORTHINESS DISCUSSION STARTER

Is it possible to regain someone's trust, once it's broken?

Explain your thinking.

TRUSTWORTHINESS DISCUSSION STARTER

How do you regain someone's trust?

Explain your thinking.

JUST SAY "NO!"

Here are some tips on how to say "NO!" if you find yourself in an uncomfortable situation with a friend or group of people.

TIP #1

Remember to firmly state your position:

For example:
   No I won't do that, that's illegal!
   No, I won't do that, that's dangerous!
   No, I won't do that, it could make me sick!

TIP #2

Suggest an alternative activity or place to go. This will make it easier for others to go along with you.

For example:
   Let's go to my house instead.
   Let's go to the park.

TIP #3

If you can't change your friend's mind, walk away but let your friend know it is their choice to join you.

For example:
   Well, I'm leaving. If you change your mind, come join me at _____.

Make a list of situations where you would say "NO!"

1.	2.
3.	4.
5.	6.
7.	8.
9.	10.

COURTESY

• Polite, considerate behaviour toward others.

Courtesy

Ask students if they know what the word courtesy or polite means. As a class, brainstorm a list of courtesy do's and don'ts. Create a class big book based on the list generated by the students.

Discussion Starters:
1. Why is it important to be polite to other people?
2. How do you feel when someone is polite to you?
3. How do you feel when you are polite?
4. How do you think others feel when you are polite to them?
5. Can you think of examples of how you can be polite to others today?

Encouraging Respect

Ask students what does it mean to treat other people with respect? Generate a class list of do's and don'ts for treating people with respect in different situations such as when there is a class visitor. Post the list up on a wall as a reminder for students. Some of the do's and don'ts may include: be courteous and polite, listen to others without interrupting, treat other people the way you want to be treated, don't give people put downs or treat them badly, and don't judge people before you get to know them.

People Are Alike, Yet Unique

Encourage students to think about how people can be alike, but still unique. Survey students on a variety of topics and create whole class graphs to demonstrate how people can be similar and/or different. Some survey ideas include: birthday months, languages spoken, favourite hobbies, and favourite foods. In addition, celebrate the differences that students have by recognizing special days in different cultures.

Discussion Starters:
1. What do they notice?
2. What surprised them?

Friendship

Ask students to define friendship and if they think they have to be a good friend to have a good friend. Create a class "recipe" of behaviors for being a good friend. Discuss each one and have students name classmates who demonstrate each behaviour. Some behaviours might be someone who: shares, is helpful, is kind, is fair, is fun or is a good sport.

Discussion Starters:
1. I think the friendship behaviour I am best at is…
2. I think the friendship behaviour I need to work on is…

RESPECTFULNESS SURVEY

People get along better when they are respectful of each other. Here are some ways you can show respect. Take this survey and think about how respectful you are of others.t

	Always	Sometimes	Never
I treat others the way I want to be treated.			
I am courteous to others and use polit words.			
I am sensitive to people's feelings.			
I treat people equally.			
I don't put people down, or embarrass them.			

Do you think you are a respectful person? Explain your thinking.

_____

_____

_____

_____

GETTING ALONG WITH OTHERS

People get along better when they cooperate and listen to each other. Take the survey and think about how well you get along with others.

Cooperation Skills

	Always	Sometimes	Never
I share things with others.			
I take turns.			
I take responsibility for my share of group work.			
I tell people when they are doing something well.			
I talk about disagreements and look for a solution.			
I invite people to join in.			

Listening Skills

	Always	Sometimes	Never
I listen to others without interrupting.			
I concentrate on what the speaker is saying.			
I ask questions to ensure understanding or to find out more.			
I look at the person while they are speaking.			
I talk about disagreements and look for a solution.			

Speaking Skills

	Always	Sometimes	Never
I speak clearly.			
I look at the person I am speaking to.			
I speak loud enough so people can hear me.			

F _____

R _____

I _____

E _____

N _____

D _____

S _____

H _____

I _____

P _____

BRAIN STRETCH: GETTING ALONG WITH OTHERS

Review your responses. How would you rate your "getting along with others" skills? Explain.

_____

_____

_____

In what ways do you need to improve?

_____

_____

_____

How do you think you can you use these skills in everyday life?

_____

_____

_____

COMPASSION

• To be sympathetic and understanding toward the needs and feelings of others.

People Have Feelings

Generate a class list of different kinds of feelings. Discuss situations that might occur around each feeling. Have students complete the "Thinking About Feelings" worksheet and discuss.

Caring People

Ask students, "What does it mean to be a caring person?" As a whole group brainstorm a list of do's and don'ts for being caring. Ask for specific examples of each behaviour they identify.

Discussion Starters:
1. How do you think a new student feels when coming to a new class?
2. What could you do to make a new student feel welcome?
3. How could you show people close to you that you care about them?

Acts Of Kindness

Brainstorm with students what it means to be kind. Record their responses on chart paper. Next go through the student generated list and have students associate the kinds of feelings they have around each act of kindness. Encourage students to understand that they have the ability to make someone happy, perhaps by complimenting them or doing something kind. Have students make compliment or appreciation cards for students in the class or create coupons to give out to people as an act of kindness.

Discussion Starters:
1. How does it feel to be kind? How does it feel to be mean?

When People Feel Angry...

Ask students to remember a time when they felt angry. Have students explain what happened and how they handled the situation. Some situations might include:

• something is unfair
• someone was mean or teased us
• something was broken
• someone is in our space
• someone is not sharing
• something has been taken away from us.

Bullying

Help students gain a clear understanding of bullying. Bullying can be described as the act of hurting someone physically or psychologically. Students should also be made aware that bullies come in all shapes and sizes. Usually someone is bullied repeatedly. Some forms of bullying include:

Physical: hitting, punching, tripping, shoving, stealing belongings, locking someone in or out etc.
Verbal: teasing, putdowns, taunting, or making embarrassing remarks etc.
Relational: excluding someone from a group, spreading rumours, or ignoring someone

It is the hope that if students can understand what a person feels like when bullied, students will develop empathy and help stop bullying.

Chalkboard Publishing © 2008

C _____

O _____

M _____

P _____

A _____

S _____

S _____

I _____

O _____

N _____

I APPRECIATE YOU!

Thank you for...

_____

_____

_____

_____

_____

_____

_____

THINKING ABOUT FEELINGS

Describe a situation that would cause each feeling.

happy	
sad	
angry	
worried	
scared	

WHAT IS BULLYING?

Bullying is when someone mistreats someone on purpose repeatedly, for example:

- name calling or put downs
- pushing or hitting
- ignoring or excluding

What 3 things can a person who is being bullied do?

1. _____

2. _____

3. _____

What are 2 things you can do if you see someone else being bullied?

1. _____

2. _____

THINKING ABOUT BULLYING

How do you think a person being bullied feels?

FEELING		WHY?
	→	

FEELING		WHY?
	→	

FEELING		WHY?
	→	

Circle in green the things you should do when bullied.

Circle in red the things you should not do when bullied.

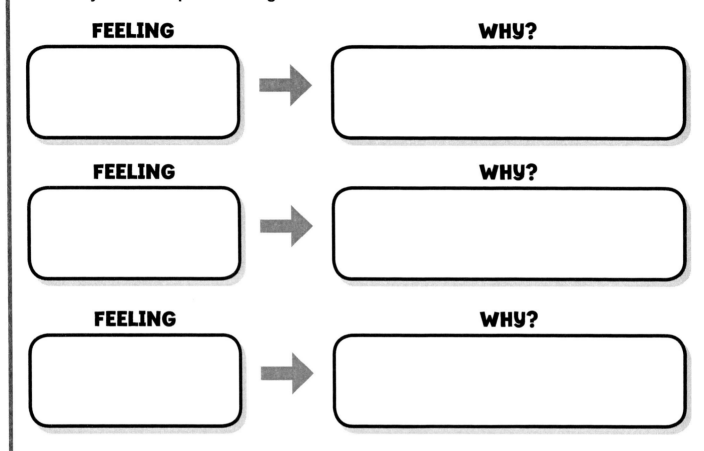

Don't tell anyone

Ignore him/her

Tell a teacher or another adult

Go to a safe place

Fight with him/her

Say you don't like it

BULLYING SCENARIOS: WHAT SHOULD YOU DO?

With a partner discuss and write a suggestion of what to do for each scenario from the perspective of: someone who is a bystander (a witness to bullying) and someone who is being bullied.

Examples of Bullying	What could a bystander do?	What could the person being bullied do?
• Making fun of what someone is wearing or how they look.		
• Shoving into someone in the hall on purpose.		
• Calling someone names.		
• Sending someone nasty emails.		
• Threatening to beat up someone if they don't do what you want		
• Making someone give you money.		
• Don't let someone sit near you even though there is enough room.		
• Spreading rumours about someone		

Chalkboard Publishing © 2008

A LETTER OF ADVICE

Choose:
- Write a letter of advice to someone who is being bullied.
- Write a letter of advice to someone who is being a bully.
- Write a letter of advice to someone who is a bystander.

Dear _____

_____

_____

_____

_____

_____

_____

_____

_____

_____

sincerely,

_____

FAIRNESS/TOLERANCE

Fairness: being truthful and just
Tolerance: respecting the individual differences, views and beliefs of other people

Fairness

Ask students what fairness means. Most people think fairness requires us to treat people equally.

1. What does treating people fairly mean?
2. Have you ever said, "That's unfair!" How do you know when something is unfair?
3. Have you ever played a game where someone has cheated? How did you feel about it?
4. Does fairness mean enforcing the same rules for everyone, even if it means losing a game?
5. What could you do when you are blamed for something you didn't do?

Honesty

As a whole group ask students what they think the expression, "honesty is the best policy" means. Do they agree with the expression? Have students explain their thinking.

Discussion Starters

1. Would you trust somebody who lies? Who cheats? Who steals? Why, or why not?
2. Have you ever told the truth, even though that was a difficult thing to do? Explain.

Sportsmanship

As a class discuss the expression, "It's not whether you win or lose its how you play the game." Brainstorm a list of ways people can show good sportsmanship. Have students create a good sportsmanship brochure using the black line master found in this teacher's guide.

Tolerance

Encourage students to understand and appreciate the differences between people. As a whole group, create a list of questions that each person in the class will respond to on the "Speed Interview Sheet". For example, What are your favourite foods? What language do you speak? What are your favourite movies? Do you have any pets? etc. Next, pair students up and have students "speed interview" each other. Have students interview as many students in the class as possible. Then, as a whole group, discuss the process and what the students discovered about each other.

Conflict Resolution Skills

Introduce the idea of conflict resolution to students. Conflict resolution is a process to help solve problems in a positive way. Each person involved is encouraged to take responsibility for their actions. Clear steps for conflict resolution might include:

- What is the problem?
- Listen without interrupting.
- Talk it out.
- Come up with different solutions.

Discuss and review the above process with students. Role-play different situations so students can practice walking through the process. Students should be encouraged to try to understand the other person's perspective of a conflict. The teacher may wish to use situations that are reflected in their class. Encourage students to come up with different solutions so they get in the habit that if a solution does not work, to try to find another one. In addition, post the steps for conflict resolution on the board for easy student reference.

Chalkboard Publishing © 2008

TOLERANCE DISCUSSION STARTERS

TOLERANCE DISCUSSION STARTER

What does it mean to be tolerant?

Give examples.

TOLERANCE DISCUSSION STARTER

Do you think there is a need for people to be more tolerant of each other?

Explain your thinking.

TOLERANCE DISCUSSION STARTER

Does tolerance mean that everyone has to agree or share the same beliefs?

Explain your thinking.

TOLERANCE DISCUSSION STARTER

Why do you think it is important to be tolerant and accept differences amongst people?

Explain your thinking.

TOLERANCE DISCUSSION STARTER

What kind of things do you think people might find difficult to tolerate?

Explain your thinking.

TOLERANCE DISCUSSION STARTER

What are the qualities of a tolerant person?

Explain your thinking.

SPEED INTERVIEW

Question	Someone who has a different answer than you.	Someone who has the same answer as you.

BRAIN STRETCH: THINKING ABOUT TOLERANCE

How do you think tolerance could make a difference in the following places?

HOME	
SCHOOL	
COMMUNITY	
WORLD	

FAIRNESS SURVEY

People get along better when they are fair with each other. Here are some ways you can show fairness. Take this survey and think about how fair you are with others.

	Always	Sometimes	Never
I treat others the way I want to be treated.			
I think about how my actions might affect others.			
I play by the rules.			
I treat people equally.			
I talk about disagreements and look for a solution.			
I admit when I am wrong.			
I show good sportsmanship.			

Do you think you are a fair person? Explain your thinking.

_____

_____

_____

_____

DEALING WITH CONFLICTS

Think of a conflict you have had recently with a friend or family member.

Describe the conflict. _____

_____

_____

_____

How did you solve this conflict? _____

_____

_____

_____

If you think there was a better way to solve this conflict, explain
what the better way would be. _____

_____

_____

_____

If you think this was the best way to solve this conflict, explain
why you feel that way. _____

_____

_____

42

WORK IT OUT!

What is the problem?

Listen without interrupting.

Talk it out.

Come up with different solutions.

Put yourself in the other person's shoes.

CITIZENSHIP

• Being law abiding and involved in service to school, community and country.

What is Citizenship?

Introduce the idea of citizenship to students in a whole group setting. Reinforce with the students that they all have something to contribute to the class, school and community.

Brainstorm a list of useful things that students could do to help out in class, at home, in the school and within the community.

Discussion Starters:

1. Ask students how they feel after they have helped someone.
2. Ask students how they feel after they have been helped.
3. Identify people who they know that volunteer at school or in the community and talk about why they do it.
4. How does obeying the rules show that you are a good citizen?
5. How do community workers make the community a better place?

Making a Difference

As a whole group brainstorm a list of people who may be in need. Encourage students to think about people they know, or situations such as children in impoverished countries. In addition, discuss charities that students might be familiar with and any fundraising activities they have participated in at school or with their families.

Give the students in your class the opportunity to practice citizenship by taking part in a school or community project. Some ideas include:

• Planting a school garden
• Collecting toys for needy children
• Collecting clothes for a shelter
• Participating in a book drive for the school or shelter
• Collecting school supplies for children in impoverished countries
• Collecting loonies for a charity
• Participating in a trash pick-up day
• Going on a class field trip to a senior citizens' home to perform songs or to sit and play games with the residents

Citizenship Class Collage

Create a class citizenship collage using words, artwork, and pictures cut out from magazines or newspapers that show examples of citizenship.

CITIZENSHIP SURVEY

People get along better when they are good citizens. Here are some ways you can show good citizenship. Take this survey and think about if you are a good citizen.

	Always	Sometimes	Never
I care about the environment.			
I take part in the school community.			
I take part in the community.			
I treat people with respect.			
I obey the law.			
I take responsibility for myself.			

Do you think you are a good citizen? Explain your thinking.

_____

_____

_____

_____

C _____

I _____

T _____

I _____

Z _____

E _____

N _____

S _____

H _____

I _____

P _____

CITIZENSHIP COLLAGE

Cut and paste pictures and words that are good examples of citizenship.

Write about your collage.

_____

_____

_____

SOMEONE I ADMIRE

Draw a picture of someone you admire.

Write about why you admire this person.

_____

_____

_____

_____

_____

_____

_____

HOW DO THESE FACTORS AFFECT YOU?

Think about your character traits. What influences have your friends, family, media, and teachers had on you as you develop attitudes about these things? Complete the chart by describing how you have been influenced in either a positive or negative manner.

FACTOR	Self-Esteem	Citizenship	Compassion
FAMILY			
FRIENDS			
MEDIA			

51

HOW DO THESE FACTORS AFFECT YOU?

Think about your character traits. What influences have your friends, family, media, and teachers had on you as you develop attitudes about these things? Complete the chart by describing how you have been influenced in either a positive or negative manner.

FACTOR	Tolerance	Courtesy	Responsibility
FAMILY			
FRIENDS			
MEDIA			

_____ 's

GOOD CHARACTER DIARY

Ideas for your diary:

- Write about the ways you have been a good citizen.
- Write about ways you have shown courtesy.
- What have you done to achieve a special goal?
- How have you shown you are responsible?
- How have you shown you are good friend?

GOOD CHARACTER DIARY
Monday

GOOD CHARACTER DIARY

Tuesday

GOOD CHARACTER DIARY

Wednesday

GOOD CHARACTER DIARY

Thursday

GOOD CHARACTER DIARY

Friday

GOOD CHARACTER DIARY

Saturday

GOOD CHARACTER DIARY

Sunday

GOOD CHARACTER TIP POSTER

Choose a character trait and create a poster about it.

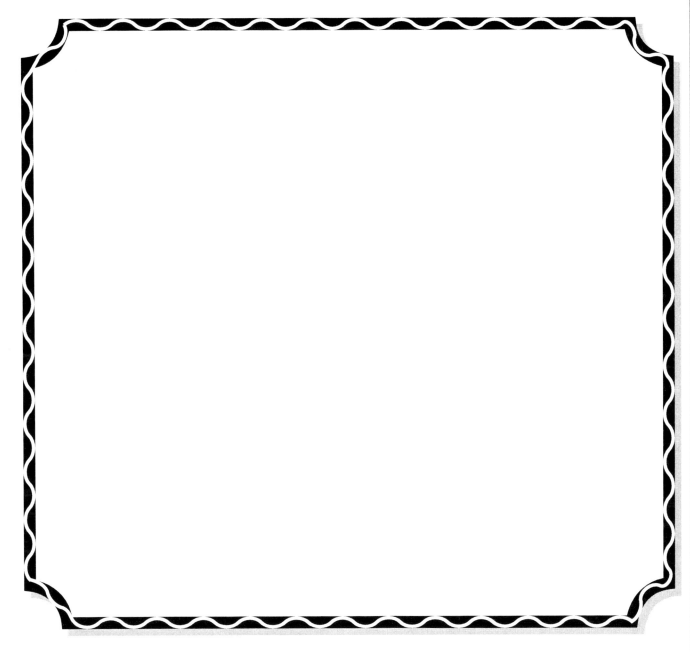

Write about your poster.

_____

_____

_____

Chalkboard Publishing © 2008

CHARACTER TRAIT CINQUAIN

A cinquain is a poem that has five lines. Follow the pattern below and write a cinquain poem about two positive character traits.

Line one: one word

Line two: two words

Line three: three words

Line four: four words

Line five: one word

Character Trait _____

Character Trait _____

COMMERCIAL CHECKLIST

Choose a positive character trait. Write a radio or TV commercial to tell people about it.

My commercial is about

_____

_____

☐ My commercial tells a clear message.

_____

_____

☐ My commercial gives reasons to support my message.

_____

_____

_____

_____

_____

_____

☐ My commercial ends with a thought to remember.

_____

_____

<u>Props</u>

☐ I used props to make my commercial interesting.

<u>Performance Style</u>

☐ I practiced and used good expression.

Chalkboard Publishing © 2008

GOOD CHARACTER BROCHURE

A *brochure* is a booklet or pamphlet that contains descriptive information. Choose a positive character trait as a topic for your brochure.

STEP 1: Plan Your Brochure

STEP	COMPLETION
1. Take a piece of paper and fold the paper the same way your brochure will be folded.	
2. • Before writing the brochure, plan the layout in pencil. • Write the heading for each section where you would like it to be in the brochure. • Leave room underneath each section to write information. • Also leave room for graphics or pictures.	

STEP 2: Complete a Draft

STEP	COMPLETION
1. Research information for each section of your brochure.	
2. Read your draft for meaning and then add, delete or change words to make your writing better.	

STEP 3: Final Editing Checklist

☐ I checked for spelling.   ☐ My brochure is neat and organized.

☐ I checked for punctuation.   ☐ My brochure has pictures or graphics.

☐ I checked for clear sentences.   ☐ My brochure is attractive.

MAGAZINE CHECKLIST

Create a magazine about positive character traits. Here is a checklist for a top quality magazine.

Magazine Cover

- [ ] The title of the magazine is easy to read and prominent on the cover.
- [ ] There is an attractive illustration to let readers know the theme of the magazine.
- [ ] There are 1 or 2 magazine highlight statements about what is inside the magazine.

Editor's Page

- [ ] The letter is addressed to the readers.
- [ ] The letter lets readers know why you think it is important to for them to read your magazine.

Table of Contents

- [ ] There is a complete listing of what is in the magazine.

Advertisements

- [ ] There are student-created advertisements throughout the magazine.

Magazine Plan:

- [ ] All the jobs on the magazine plan are complete.

Brain Stretch:

Make a list of article ideas, advertisements or other things that you make include in your magazine.

| |
| |
| |
| |
| |

Chalkboard Publishing © 2008

MAGAZINE PLAN

Group Members: _____

_____

Job	Group Member	Complete

WRITE A MAGAZINE ARTICLE

Pretend you are a reporter for Good Character! Magazine. Write an article to help students understand the importance and benefits of displaying good character. Some ideas you may wish to write about include:

- A Person You Admire
- The Importance of Taking Responsibility For Your Own Actions
- How One Person Who Shows Citizenship Can Make A Difference

These are the parts of an article you need to know:

- The **HEADLINE** names the article.
- The **BYLINE** shows the name of the author. (You)
- The **BEGINNING** gives the most important idea.
- The **MIDDLE** gives supporting details about the idea.
- The **ENDING** usually gives the reader an idea to remember.

Article Checklist:

Content

☐ I have a HEADLINE that names the article.

☐ I have a BYLINE that shows my name as the author.

☐ I have a BEGINNING that gives the most important facts.

☐ I have a MIDDLE part that tells details about the article.

☐ I have an ENDING that gives the reader an idea to remember.

Grammar and Style

☐ I used my neatest printing and included a clear title

☐ I included a colourful picture

☐ I spelled my words correctly

☐ I used interesting words

☐ I checked for capitals, periods, commas and question marks

Chalkboard Publishing © 2008

A WEB ABOUT...

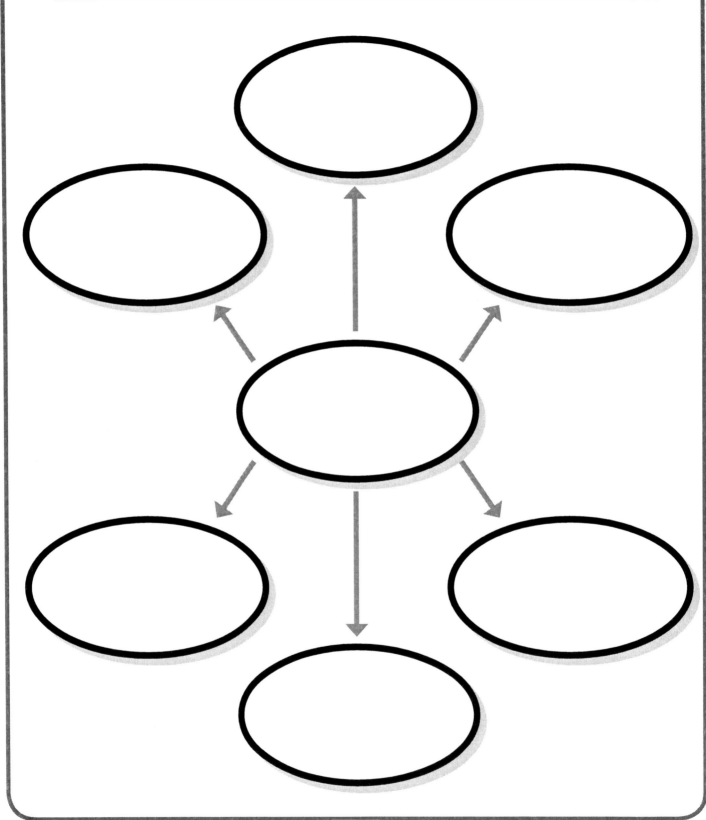

SHOWING GOOD CHARACTER

Give an example of how someone could demonstrate each good character trait.

CITIZENSHIP

PERSEVERANCE

COURTESY

RESPONSIBILITY

SPORTSMANSHIP

SHOWING GOOD CHARACTER

Give an example of how someone could demonstrate each good character trait.

FAIRNESS

COOPERATION

TOLERANCE

COMPASSION

PRIDE

Chalkboard Publishing © 2008

CHARACTER TRAIT WORD SEARCH

T	C	O	M	P	A	S	S	I	O	N	S	E	J	U	A
D	R	W	R	B	I	Q	R	A	L	S	U	K	L	S	N
I	T	U	E	C	D	H	M	E	E	U	Y	T	P	D	N
L	Q	H	S	F	H	P	S	N	S	U	D	O	N	O	Q
I	S	O	P	T	I	A	D	N	B	P	R	N	I	N	M
G	S	N	O	E	W	N	R	I	E	T	E	T	O	T	E
E	E	E	N	G	I	O	W	A	S	Z	A	C	O	R	E
N	N	S	S	K	L	Y	R	M	C	R	I	L	T	S	T
C	R	T	I	M	D	U	A	T	E	T	E	T	P	U	S
E	I	Y	B	Z	B	N	H	P	H	R	E	R	I	Z	E
O	A	Y	I	V	S	R	O	N	A	I	I	R	D	C	F
N	F	I	L	H	V	O	P	N	Z	D	N	K	K	U	L
W	P	K	I	G	C	G	C	I	E	X	X	E	L	L	E
T	C	P	T	Y	S	E	T	R	U	O	C	P	S	B	S
U	O	A	Y	Y	P	O	S	I	T	I	V	E	D	S	V
E	C	N	A	R	E	V	E	S	R	E	P	M	V	X	R

Find the words listed below in the word search. Hint: some words may be spelled backwards!

character	cooperation	fairness
citizenship	courtesy	honesty
compassion	diligence	kindness
respect	sportsmanship	perseverance
responsibility	tolerance	positive
self-esteem	trustworthiness	pride

Write a character trait in the centre of the flower. In the petals, give examples of the character trait.

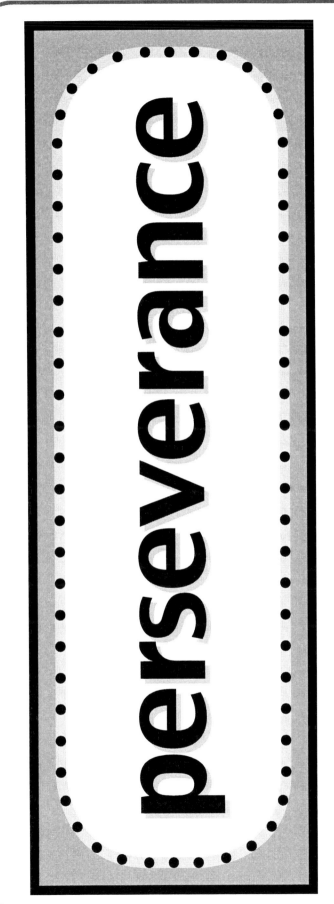

perseverance

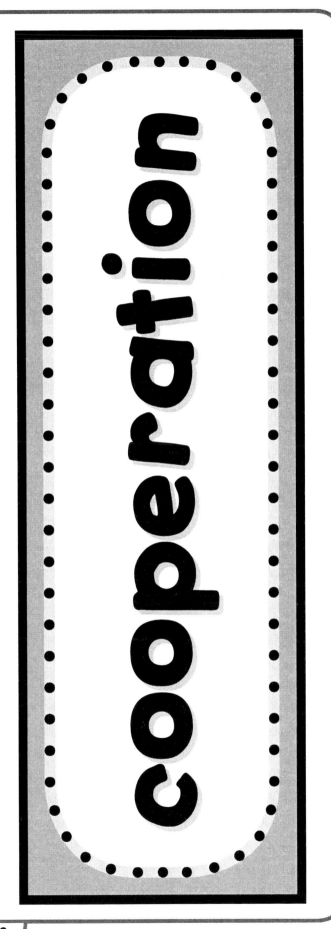

coopperation

69

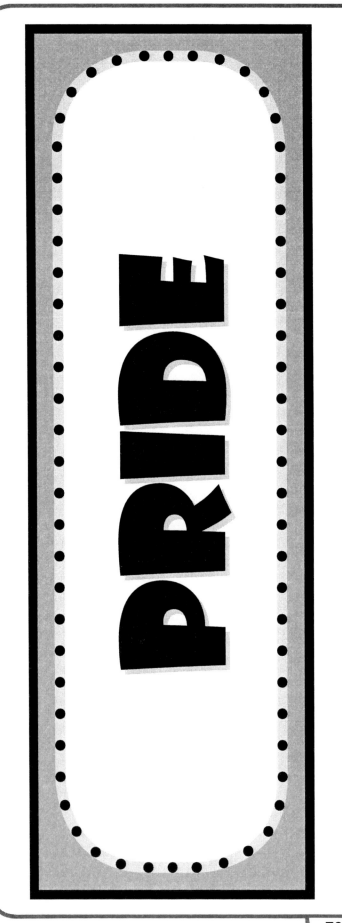

70

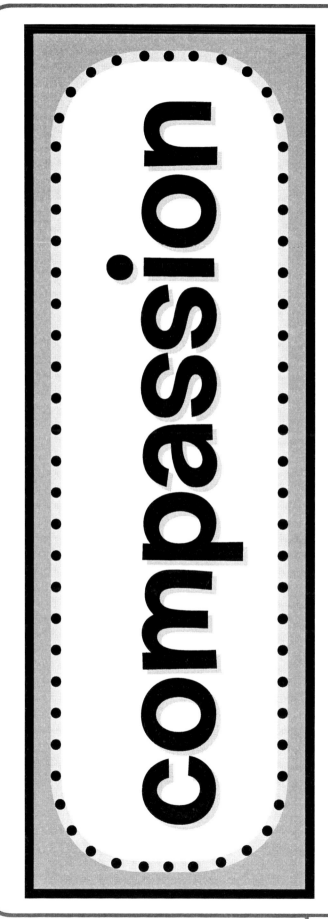

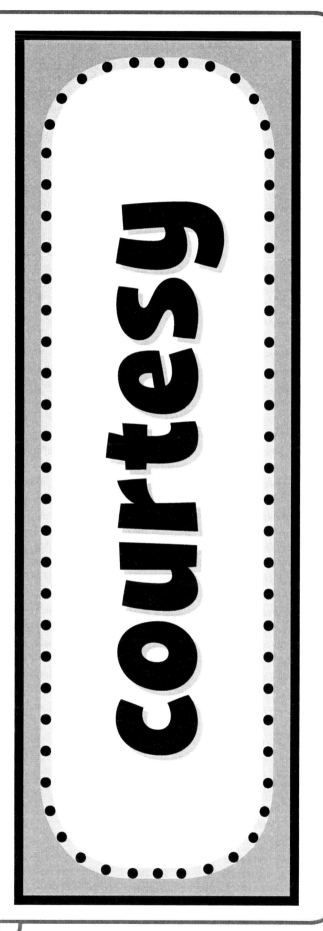

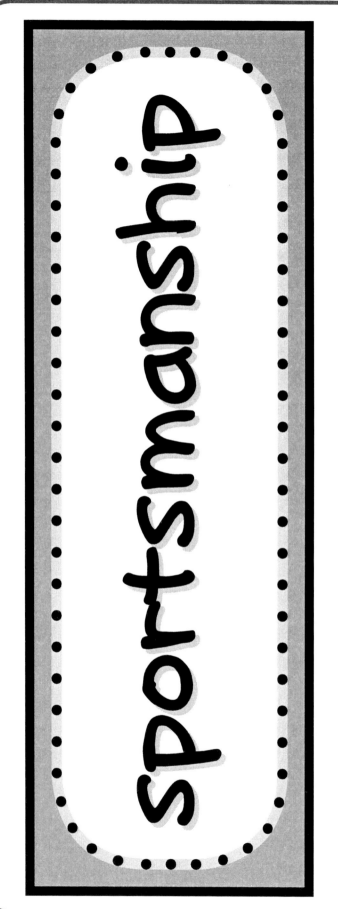

sportsmanship

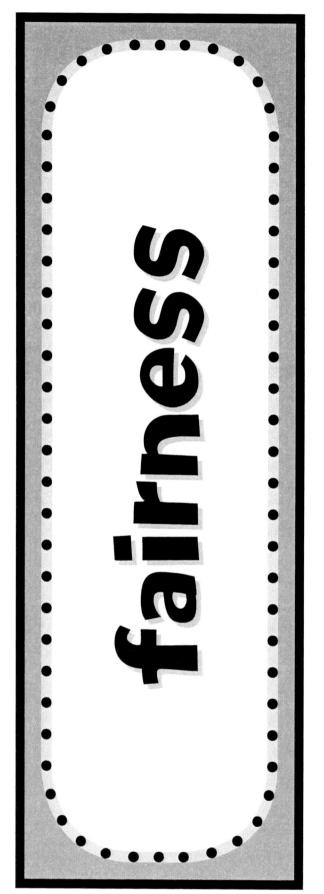

fairness

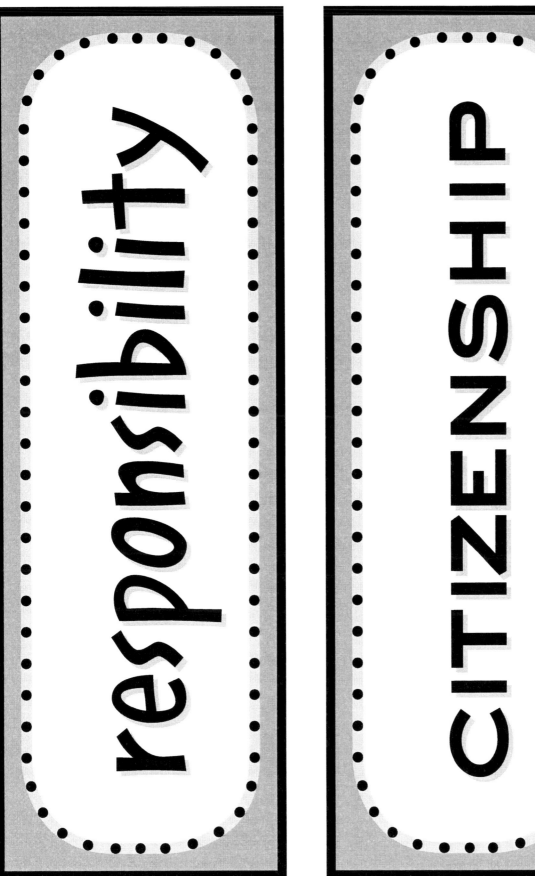

responsibility

CITIZENSHIP

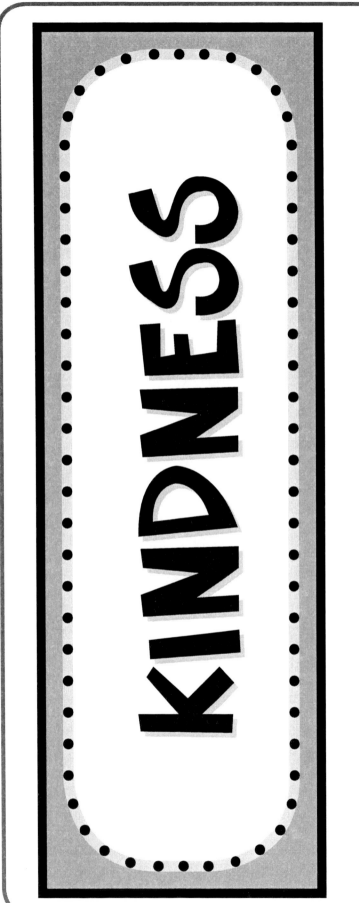

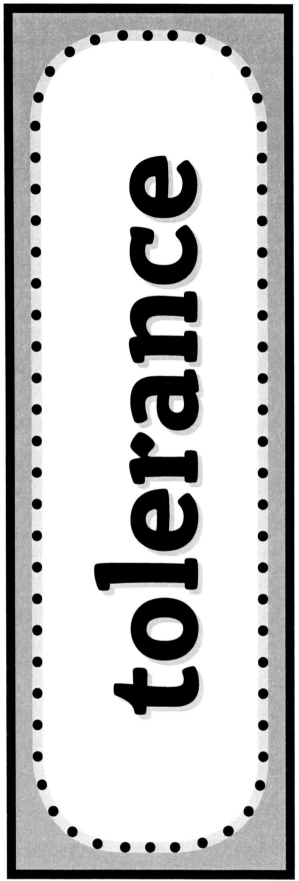

RESPONSIBILITY AWARD

Keep up the effort!

GREAT FRIEND AWARD

This award is for:

_____

COURTESY AWARD

KEEP UP THE EFFORT!

TOP MANNERS!

THIS AWARD IS FOR:

_____

GREAT JOB!

Keep up the effort!

SUPER SPORTSMANSHIP!

This award is for:

_____

CITIZENSHIP 🍁 AWARD 🍁

KEEP UP
THE EFFORT!

Community Helper AWARD

This award is for

_____

STUDENT PARTICIPATION RUBRIC

LEVEL	STUDENT PARTICIPATION DESCRIPTOR
Level 4	Student consistently contributes to class discussions and activities by offering ideas and asking questions.
Level 3	Student usually contributes to class discussions and activities by offering ideas and asking questions.
Level 2	Student sometimes contributes to class discussions and activities by offering ideas and asking questions.
Level 1	Student rarely contributes to class discussions and activities by offering ideas and asking questions.

UNDERSTANDING OF CONCEPTS RUBRIC

LEVEL	UNDERSTANDING OF CONCEPTS DESCRIPTOR
Level 4	Student shows a thorough understanding of all or almost all concepts and consistently gives appropriate and complete explanations independently. No teacher support is needed.
Level 3	Student shows a good understanding of most concepts and usually gives complete or nearly complete explanations. Infrequent teacher support is needed.
Level 2	Student shows a satisfactory understanding of most concepts and sometimes gives appropriate, but incomplete explanations. Teacher support is sometimes needed.
Level 1	Student shows little of understanding of concepts and rarely gives complete explanations. Intensive teacher support is needed.

COMMUNICATION OF CONCEPTS RUBRIC

LEVEL	COMMUNICATION OF CONCEPTS DESCRIPTOR
Level 4	Student consistently communicates with clarity and precision in written and oral work. Student consistently uses appropriate terminology and vocabulary.
Level 3	Student usually communicates with clarity and precision in written and oral work. Student usually uses appropriate terminology and vocabulary.
Level 2	Student sometimes communicates with clarity and precision in written and oral work. Student sometimes uses appropriate terminology and vocabulary.
Level 1	Student rarely communicates with clarity and precision in written and oral work. Student rarely uses appropriate terminology and vocabulary.

Chalkboard Publishing © 2008

HOW AM I DOING?

	COMPLETING MY WORK	USING MY TIME WISELY	FOLLOWING DIRECTIONS	KEEPING ORGANIZED
FULL SPEED AHEAD!	• My work is consistently complete and done with care • I added extra details to my work	• I consistently get my work done on time	• I consistently follow directions	• My materials are consistently neatly organized • I am consistently prepared and ready to learn
KEEP GOING!	• My work is complete and done with care • I checked over my work	• I usually get my work done on time	• I usually follow directions without reminders	• I usually can find my materials • I am usually prepared and ready to learn
SLOW DOWN!	• My work is complete • I need to check over my work	• I sometimes get my work done on time	• I sometimes need reminders to follow directions	• I sometimes need time to find my materials • I am sometimes prepared and ready to learn
STOP!	• My work is not complete • I need to check over my work	• I rarely get my work done on time	• I need reminders to follow directions	• I need to organize my materials • I am rarely prepared and ready to learn